SERMONS

ON RECENT

NATIONAL VICTORIES,

AND THE

NATIONAL SORROW.

PREACHED, APRIL 23D, 1865,

IN THE PLYMOUTH CHURCH,

By the Pastor, E. P. POWELL.

Adrian, Mich.,

SMITH & FOSTER, PRINTERS, OPPOSITE LAWRENCE HOTEL.

1865.

SERMON,

APPROPRIATE TO THE OBSEQUIES OF ABRAHAM LINCOLN.

JOHN 11, 50.—"Consider that it is expedient for us that one man should die for the people, and that the whole Nation perish not."

May 18th, 1860, the American people met at Chicago, by Delegates, to elect a Candidate to rule over twenty-five degrees of latitude and sixty degrees of longitude. Thirty millions of people, recognizing the fact that liberty can be preserved only under due restraints, sought voluntarily a Chief Magistrate. They looked at McLean, who, among our Judges was in wisdom dignity and judgment, Chief before the Chief Justice.

They looked at William H. Seward, who was, without doubt, the choice of a majority of the Republican party.—Seward had led us as no other Statesman ever did. Clay was the peoples friend, Webster the peoples defender, Jefferson the peoples oracle, Jackson the peoples pride; but history will write that William H. Seward, during the first century of American Independence, was the real peoples leader. Never going but one point ahead of us, he patiently waited for his logic to take its effect, and the people were sure to come up to him; then onward just one step more, and he waited for us to take the same step, and take it we did. He gave us our political passwords; and in twenty-five years induced more progress in political views than perhaps all other Statesmen from Hamilton down to the present. Men with the same views achieved nothing with the popular will, because they were only agitators. As radical as Phillips or Garrison, Seward led the people, while Phillips strove to drive them. Yet the

Convention passed by Seward, in their choice for President. Old men who loved his greatness and gloried in his strength, sat down like children and wept.

They looked to Attorney General Bates. In him some saw the model gentleman, who by a wise conservatism, reserved dignity, and soundness of judgment would be just the man to combine conflicting elements. He was to be the oil on the waters of threatened secession. But they passed by Bates.

They looked, I am sorry to add, at Simon Cameron, the Simon Magus of American politics.

All these were men of note, ability, and great personal and political strength. But it was as when Samuel was sent to the family of Jesse to anoint a King over Israel. Eliab passed before him, and he said surely this is the Lords anointed. But the Lord said look not on his countenance, for the Lord seeth not as man seeth; for man looketh on the outward appearance; but the Lord looketh on the heart. And nine other sons passed by, but the Lord refused them all. But David the youngest was tending sheep, and when the prophet insisted on his being sent for, the Lord said This is he, anoint him.

Thus our old leaders and Statesmen were passed by, and the people invited to give their suffrages to Abraham Lincoln. The name was somewhat familiar to the American people, as that of the only man on the prairies who could face Stephen A. Douglas. The choice was simply a direction of Providence. Lincoln never would have been the choice of the majority of voters, had not a Convention first selected him. Seward, or Chase, or McLean were decidedly more in popular favor. A man who never in his life received but one years school education; a farm boy chopping a clearing in the forest at ten; a hired hand on a river flat boat at nineteen; at twenty-one a rail splitter, living in a log cabin of his own building; at twenty-two a boat builder, at twelve dollars a month; at twenty-four a store keeper, and poor at that; at twenty-five a Postmaster; at twenty-six a Surveyor; at twenty-seven a member of the Legislature; at twenty-eight a Lawyer; at thirty-five Presidential Elector; at thirty-seven a Representative in Congress; at fifty-one President of the the Uuited States.

He was not the first choice of the people; but he was the

choice of God. A work was to be done, which we can see now, no man could or would have achieved, as has Lincoln. A keener Statesman would have had his preconceived views, and endeavored to compel events to develop in a given channel. The glory of this Administration is that it has not inquired of precedents, but moved with the movements of Providence. Lincoln taught us a new rule of statesmanship "The Logic of Events," and the most hopeful indication of the new Administration is, that President Johnson declares he shall be guided by the same rule. The man who should have striven to guide the past four years, by previous years, would have ruined us. Seward with that keenness of intellect that cleaves marble, had his party ties, his preconceived views, and would probably have run afoul of Providence.

The work to be done was to watch the foul fiend of Slavery in its death struggle; to hold the helm of State in a most terrible civil war; to proclaim liberty to the captive; to enshrine himself in the hearts of his people next to Washington; and after a laborious, saddening Administration in the hour of victory, alas to *die* for his people and his country.

The character of our departed President was new; it was a western American conglomerate, petrified by trial into a marble as hard and pure as that of Paros. He was a western Yankee. Losing the penuriousness of the Yankee who delves the rocks of Connecticut; made generous by the fertility of the prairies, his mind widened out to a broader scope by the rich valleys of our great rivers, the western Yankee adds a quaint coat of mail to his character—a humor that protects him from the wear of business and care. Lincoln was a representative man of the Great West. His humor, scorned by the sedater statesman, looked on at first distrustfully by the patriot, no doubt saved him from being crushed with anxiety and labor. We could not, and cannot appreciate how terrible a weight, we as the American people, placed on his shoulders; nor how providential was that minute trait of character that stood by him to lift the heavy helmet from his brain. When Kings used to rule, instead of having Ministers to rule for them they relieved themselves by retaining at Court a humorous jester to stir them to laughter. The humor of Lincoln was the Kings fool of his character; but it bore him as important a part as his sedater judgment.

Another prominent and even remarkable characteristic of the deceased was his kindliness of disposition. He seemed truly born to be the *Father of a Nation.*

"Tyrant!" He was the last man in America to be styled tyrant. His soul was as gentle as Cowper's, or the Apostle John's. He was incapable of ill will. Only his oath and his duty ever made him the helmsman in a time of war. And it was just this grand royal benevolence of heart, that made his assassination the death of the Rebellion. We were just about to follow his beloved guidance to an amnesty, we fear. Far sighted lovers of their country had only one fear, that the one who had steered through the sea of war, might not weather the breakers along the shore of peace. Would it do to pardon treason? Could we, as was hinted, "afford to be generous?" The old ship of the Confederacy was surely sinking; would it do to calk it, if only they would run up the Stars and Stripes, and set ashore their cargo of slaves? We knew their ship was not far from sinking, when that crafty old Mississippi rat, Hangman Foote, took to the water. It seemed more certain when Hunter, Stephens and Campbell ran out the white flag, saying, "let us negotiate." The fate of the Rebellion was still more certain as we heard the tramp of Sherman, storming States and outflanking the Alleghanies. But when Davis fled, and Lee surrendered, and Richmond was ours, we began to remember the goodness of the Presidents heart, and we feared that after all, Davis might not sink. But, my friends, they scuttled their own ship, when they shot Abraham Lincoln. We know now their doom. Amnesty is no longer thought of for wholesale murderers. The nation, almost unanimously, shouts down to that world where God consigns *his* rebels, saying, make way down there for your friends; prepare for those who cannot find a government good enough on this globe. His secnod Administration found Lincoln a largely different man from what the first found him. He was battered by Providences into a nobler and deeper character. He had learned a wider grasp of Statesmanship; and above all he had learned that his only hope was in God. What could be our consolation, if we did not feel that we should meet our dear President among the saved of Jesus. Sweet to us are those treasured words of his, "I love Jesus."

Probably almost every mind in the country, classes Lincoln with Washington. For some reason they seem nearer each other than any other two Presidents; unless it be Adams and Jefferson. Adams and Jefferson were the two Philosophers and Statesmen: Washington and Lincoln the two Fathers of their country. Alike, and yet largely unlike, each led us through a great peril; and with a wisdom born of a pure heart, more than of a great brain. Each was bitterly belied in his life, but unanimously lamented in his death, even by those he had conquered. Each was elected to a second term of office; and that too by a spontaneous outburst of national confidence. Yet were they unlike in this; Washington was a creative genius, out of chaos producing a stable government, a government unique and wonderful. Lincoln lacked the constructive power, and waited that affairs might shape themselves. Washington was his superior in the finished courtesies of life, but not in the kindliness of his nature. Equal in patriotism, equal in purity, Lincoln stands second only to the Father of his Country. And now as we look back over his Administration, we find little that we cannot approve: we find nothing to blame. God led him, and he was willing, after a while, to be led. When he erred, he erred less than would others; when he did wisely, he did it with his heart as well as his pen. Oh how much have we to thank God, that in the hour of trial he gave us a real patriot, never selfish, never untrue to his country. How terribly in his power should we lie, if some ambitious unscrupulous man were President, with such an army at his command.

But no one, ever for a moment, distrusted Lincoln. Meekly he bore his honors.. For his country he thought, for his country ruled; and with the almost visible care and presence of God, he led us through the darkest hours, full up to the dawn of peace, with all the love of the nation centered in him, and then in the very hour of triumph, when we thought him for the first time safe, just returned from a visit to the charnel house of secession, the horrable deed was done. May we never again suffer what we suffered one week ago. The word flew on the telegraphic wire, "The President is shot." I shall never forget the sickening effect of those words. But we loved him. Yet he is—dead. But who could gain by it? Yet he is dead. Vengeance on the assassin we cried! But that will not restore our dear President to life. Like Rachel mourning for her children, we would not be comforted for *he* was not. He had a right to reap the fruit of his labors. But he cannot! Dead! Dead! Would to God I had died for thee! Oh Lincoln! My Father! My Father! Assassinated! Oh how an American hates that cowardly word. Henceforth he will hate it with a double detestation.

But alas we needed the blow. We needed it to waken us to the horrid nature of treason. We were so tired of war that we were willing to buy peace at a sacrifice of justice and safety. We needed it to unite the people, and under a common loss, to bind us for a common effort. We needed it to rouse the whole loyal heart against northern sympathy for treason—the diabolical spirit that could rejoice in assassination. We needed it to illustrate the fiendishness and fury of arch rebels. We needed it to shame every decent man in the South, and make him blush for his cause. We needed it to make us rely on God, and not on an arm of flesh. We needed it as a punishment for our terrible wickedness, in insulting God for all the preceding victories.

"With silence only as their benediction,
  God's angels come;
When in the shadow of a great affliction
  The soul sits dumb.

Yet would we say what every heart approveth,
  Our Fathers will,
Calling to Him, the dear one whom he loveth,
  Is mercy still.

Not upon us, or ours, the solemn angel,
  Hath EVIL wrought,
The funeral anthem is a glad evangel,
  The good die not.

God called our President; but we lose not wholly
  What he had given:
He lives on Earth in thought and deed, as truly
  As in His Heaven."

We needed it to teach us how to curse the Spirit of Slavery. Frequently during this war we have read great rewards offered for the assasination of Lincoln, Seward, Beecher, Greeley, Butler. Only last December one southern paper published the following: "One million dollars wanted to have peace by the first of March. If the citizens of the Southern Confederacy will furnish me with the cash, or good securities for one million dollars, I will cause the lives of Abraham Lincoln, William H. Seward, and Andrew Johnson to be taken by the 1st of March." What land, but one, whose inhabitants were often stained with the blood of murdered slaves would have tolerated such an offer. It was more than probable that the act was paid for according to the terms here demanded. Not Booth alone killed our President; but every man who has cherished a spirit of lawlessness, all who have sympathized with the murderous spirit of slavery.

In the soul of the perpetrator there seems to have been blended such elements as these: the child of illegality, himself licentious, and therefore heartless, he was callous to finer nobler emotions. Sympathy with tyranny had taught him to hate all who stood in his way. Familiarity with acting murders, had robed crime with romance, and made assassination a play. Criminal habits left him always in the need of money, and ready to be bought for villany. But the power that finally developed, and made active, all these elements, was the demon of slavery. Stop my friends and think what a viper of treason and fury we have fed in our country's bosom. Fear. ful in its life; devouring daily the happiness of four millions, their liberty and their labors; often drinking their blood, and making music of their lamentations; yet in its death is slave ry most fearful of all.

When Herod was about to die, he invited to his palace, all the distinguished men of his Kingdom. When they were gathered, he ordered them flung into dungeons, and as soon as he should die, that they be all slaughtered; for, said he, the people *shall* mourn for me—I will make them dread my dying more than living. Slavery saw its death approaching, and its fiendish spirit determined to leave behind a nation of mourners. It has well succeeded. Look for a moment at the horrible grandeur of its mausoleum. At least two millions of corpses—stark and bloody, cemented with the tears of thirty millions. But that was not enough. It must strike a more shining mark; and with what we hope is its last struggle. It has assassinated the President. That is what this domestic institution has cost us. It is the hand of God. We deserved it—and bow down in tears and prayer.

And yet this great nation owes it to itself not to give way to despair. We have lost our President, but we have not lost our God. At the best Lincoln could not have lived but a few years; but He who founded our nation, and has sustained it from Washington to Lincoln, is not only the same yesterday and to-day, but forever. Spanning over administrations of comparative insignificance. He will give us again, in the future, other glorious names to be linked with the Father and Savior of his country. Or, perhaps, he has in store for us, a succession of administrations as pure and renowned, as those just preceding them have been disgraceful and selfish.

It is pleasantly consoling to think that our great friend suffered less, than if he had been prostrated by a long illness.—It was the nation that felt the bullet, and bore the suffering.—Lincoln knew nothing of his passage, till awaking in another life, some angel told him the story of his murder. He who had lived so well for his country, God granted to die also for his country. He lived valuably, he died valuably. As we look back at the fruit of his life, we are at a loss to know, if after all, his martyrdom may not prove of still greater value.

Had he died a few months sooner, he would have gone when the heats of partisan strife had maligned him. Had the plot to assassinate him succeeded on the fourth of March, it would have been before the fruit of his administrative labors had become manifest, we should not have known just how to estimate him. There is a time in every earnest noble life, when its work is just complete. Happy the man who dies then.—Lincoln died without having unravelled a single thread of the good he had accomplished. Had he lived a few weeks more, he might, in the kindliness of his disposition, have misjudged the needs of the time, and ruined much, that a firmer hand would have compacted and strengthened.

He was killed just when party strife had been dissipated—when victory had made us more kindly disposed, and his death could bind the nation in a new vow of brotherhood. Victories made us laugh together. His murder has made us weep together. Our tears have washed out party lines. I think that even thousands of the rebels must be more than converted to loyalty, by discovering the fiendish climax of their paricide. They who could stab their Government, must shudder when they see the logical result of their action.

With anxious hearts we now turn to the man who is given us to fill the place of Lincoln. We turn with suspicious questionings, and some doubts; and yet with a holier faith that God does not intend to cast us off; but to call us closer to Himself.

Andrew Johnson is, we trust, a man that will yet be loved as purely and fondly as Abraham Lincoln. He has already declared the opening of a new policy—a sterner adhesion to justice. And why not? weakness, when the nation is in danger, is only thirty million times as evil as indecision when a single person's safety is involved. As a minister of the gospel of peace, I cannot see why we should pardon all treason.—Suppose we assure amnesty to all murderers, burglars and assassins. Our lives would soon be too cheap to be worth care. To proclaim an amnesty to traitors, is to offer a bounty on treason. Those who have seen the most of the Rebellion are the best judges of its cure. When General Sherman was in Savannah, one of the unterrified said to him, "General you may conquer, but you can't subjugate us." He instantly replied, "I don't wan't to subjugate you, I mean to kill you, the whole of you, if you don't stop this rebellion." Another wanted to know how long the war would last "Well, well," said Sherman, "I don't know, perhaps six or eight years; then twenty or twenty-five years of guerrilla warfare,—long enough to destroy this whole generation, and then we'll begin anew."

Our President says destroy the leaders, and spare the led.—

Hang the intelligent managers, and send home the ignorant masses, with Yankee school-masters behind them. It seems as if God had raised up Andrew Johnson, fitting him from his very birth, to be the American Hercules, to cleanse the Angean stables of Slavery, and strangle the Nemean lion of Secession.

Lincoln was not a leader, but a servant of the people; Johnson is a leader. He has had practical experience in statesmanship and government; he will need it all now. He has met and understands Jefferson Davis, and the Southern leaders. He it was, that faced them four years ago in the Senate, and craved the power to hang their traitorous necks. He is the second Andrew of Tennessee. We have prayed for Andrew Jackson. God has given us Andrew Johnson. He understands the South. He has been through the fire. No man like him could have restored Tennessee and brought it out for freedom. There is in the Bible a caution to put on that armor that will enable us to stand against the *wiles* of the devil.—Lincoln could meet the old Devil of Secession in fair fight. Johnson can better detect him in his wily conferences. He is, like Lincoln, a peoples man; from the people—having no sympathy with aristocracy, and even greater simplicity of manners. He has equal goodness of heart, and greater firmness. God grant he may prove the Franklin of Presidents.

It is strange that General Grant, who now is supreme in war, and President Johnson, who now is supreme in peace, should have both been denounced as drunkards. And yet each has been thoroughly exonerated, by abundant testimony. It was well that each had a warning at the outset. One, who was in Congress with Mr. Johnson, says: "I knew him well, and I assure my countrymen that no man can be found of more correct habits or principles. He is the friend of the people and the enemy of their oppressors." Another writes: "I have known him intimately for twenty years. During his public life at Washington, I have been in his room hundreds of times. I never saw a drop of liquor there, on any occasion; never saw him drink a drop—never had reason to believe that he ever tasted it." You have all probably seen the testimony of General Burnside; who says: "We met at all hours of the day and night, and I never saw him taste liquor, nor ever saw him when he had tasted liquor. He was no drunkard then, and in my opinion is a firm, loyal and talented statesman."

Thank God for this testimony! Rid of this one fear, the American people can trust their hopes, under God, to this new comer, with confidence. We never doubted his will and his heart; we do not now doubt his moral character. With this hope in the coming man, we rouse onrselves from the gloom of despair, and set to our work.

He that we loved is gone, but God is still with us. In him is our chief hope. If we bear this stroke from him with a will to obey, to turn from our sins, and act righteously, our future shall surely be grander than the imagination can paint.

And now, Abraham Lincoln we bid thee a tender farewell. It is because we owe thee, under God, so great a debt that we mourn for thee so deeply. If tears would restore thee, surely this nation would call thee back. We do what we can; we go down in sad procession to accompany thee to the borders of another life. Three millions of freedmen come after thee, chanting God bless Massa Lincoln. Twenty millions of free-born come kneeling at thy grave, God bless our dear President! One hundred thousand mothers who gave their boys; one hundred thousand wives who gave their husbands; five hundred thousand orphans that gave their fathers, come, and without exception, pray, Oh God bless him who so loved and cared for our sons and fathers.

One man was found in all America, who could kill him. Millions would die to restore him to life.

Requiem,

FOR PRESIDENT ABRAHAM LINCOLN.

" Now wake the requiem's solemn moan,
For him whose patriot task is done!
A Nation's heart stands still to-day
With horror, o'er his martyred clay!

O, God of Peace, repress the ire,
Which fills our souls with vengeful fire!
Vengeance is thine, and Sovereign might,
Alone, can such a crime requite!

Farewell,thou good and guileless heart!
The manliest tear for thee must start!
E'en those at times who blamed thee here,
Now deeply sorrow o'er thy bier!

O Jesus, grant him sweet repose,
Who seemed, like thee, to love his foes!
Those foes, like thine, their wrath to spend,
Have slain their best, their firmest friend."

GLORIA.

Praise God from whom all blessings flow!
Praise him all sorrowing hearts below!
Praise him above, ye martyred host,
Praise Father, Son and Holy Ghost.

SERMON,

APPROPRIATE TO THE OBSEQUIES OF JEFFERSON DAVIS, AND THE SOUTHERN CONFEDERACY.

ROMANS, 9, 17.—"The Scripture saith unto Pharaoh; even for this same purpose have I raised thee up, that I might show my power in thee, and that my name might be declared in all the earth."

Every man is raised up for a purpose. Pharaoh, though as free to become the emancipator of the Israelites, was nevertheless an example of stubborn resistance to what seemed inevitable; a vain conceited believer in his own omnipotence; bringing ruin upon himself and his people, by his arrogant resistance to God. It was evident that the days of Hebrew slavery were ended; yet Pharaoh endured plagues upon his person, on his neighbors, on crops and trees, on revenue, on cattle, and on the lives of all the first born, before he would obey the command to "let my people go." And after they had even departed, he pursued them down into the Red Sea, and met the fate that he deserved—the death of a fool.

Now in our own day, God has raised up the precise after-type of Pharaoh; Jefferson Davis, the Chairman of the late Confederate States.

A better King in Egypt would have delayed the emancipation of the Israelites. A better Senator than Jefferson Davis would have delayed the emancipation of America. His object was certainly anything but pious or patriotic, yet, like Pharaoh, his very madness God overruled for glorious and good ends.

A believer in Calhounism; first, a repudiator of State debts, he grew in wickedness as he grew in years, until he said: Go to now, let us destroy this great American Union, and get to ourselves a great name. Let us establish a Confederacy of aristocracy, where we may rule perpetually. Its corner stone shall be African slavery; its Kings shall be I and mine forever. His object was to aggrandize himself; to perpetuate human slavery; to get free from the irritation of honest industry, and equality with northern mechanics. To do this he would plot, steal, destroy, repudiate, *secede*. He thought to take off one half of our territory, and make it a private possession. There were others equally wicked and guilty, but Davis by common consent, was foremost of the guilty crew. This was *his* plan—but the Lord God had another. The Almighty heard the cry of four millions of bondsmen pleading, Oh Lord! how long? how long?—Massa Jesus come to deliver? He saw the finest part of America blighted by slavery; its streams, that might have been lined with Lowells and Lynns, idly rolling to the sea. Its inhabitants starving with aristocracy, and besotted with inertness; few schools, and those taught by Northerners; its soil being exhausted by ignorance, and desolation creeping over the whole. God meant to put a new soul into the South; to give it hands that could work; heads that could think, and hearts that could feel. He meant to open the mill-streams to Yankee inventions, and send district schools into the sunny valleys. He meant to commingle this great nation, and abolish Mason's and Dixon's line; to show the poor whites of the South what fools they were in hating Yankees; to end the long discussion concerning slavery; to preach deliverance to the captive, and to let the oppressed go free. And He meant that Jefferson Davis should be the main instrument in doing it. You say *Lincoln.* No Lincoln did not go one step farther than Davis compelled him.

To accomplish this work of the Lord, needed a peculiar man. He must first be ambitious—ravened with a desire to rule. He must be proudly obstinate, so as to hold on to the end. He must be able and cunning, in order to lead the South. He must be unscrupulous in ways and means. He must be an overbearing aristocrat,—the exact and complete type of slaveholding aristocracy. It needed a man who could organize and consummate a terrible rebellion; who would not hesitate to shed rivers of blood, and wade through it to power; a man who could gloat in the ruin of his country, the defilement of its flag, the misery of its mothers; and rejoice in the prospect of the carnage and plunder of Northern cities. All this was found in Jefferson Davis. Slavery must die in such a way as to make its death its worst curse, that hereafter it might lie under the execrations of the whole human race.

Such was the work that Davis planned—such also the work evidently planned for him. Now let us see what he achieved, and how well he did it.

His reign has continued for about four years. At the beginning of that period, there were fifteen States in which slavery was soundly intrenched. It was estimated that it could not be driven from them under half a century. Even Lincoln, at his inauguration, distinctly declared his inability, by right, to interfere with State Institutions. Had it not been for Davis, he never would have touched them. But thanks to aristocratic Davis, the work of fifty years has been achieved in four. Human bondage is a shadow, where it exists in name. The Emancipation Proclamation trembled long on Lincoln's pen, but every victory of the South made it more a necessity. And the Lord hardened Davis' heart, till the contraband *thing* began to be a trench-digger; and the spade-user grew up into a musket-holder; and at last a negro regiment marched into Richmond singing John Brown. John Brown's soul has been more troublesome than his body, and what is worse it can't be hung. It marched to Missouri and made it a free State; to Maryland, to West Virginia, to Tennessee, and set up everywhere new and free governments. It stopped at Governor Wise's parlor and opened a negro school.

Four years ago the sound of war was just breaking over us; and we shuddered to think of our prosperity, our commerce, all under the blight of blood shedding. We dreaded to think of the future. Fort Sumpter was the first scene; Bull Run bloody, disastrous, terrifying, was the second; Ball's Bluff, Shiloh, the Peninsula grave-digging succeeded. Buell's blunders, McClellan's indecisions, Halleck's lines of circumvalla tion in the swamps of Corinth,—which ended in taking the village, but nobody in it; all these sickened us. Then came the treachery that ruined Pope and defeated Burnside. Generals bidding for the enemies votes for President; pirates ruining our commerce. But what a magnificent change has four years wrought. Gettysburg, Chattanooga, New Orleans, Mobile, Wilmington; Sherman's circumnavigation of Secessia; Grant's garroting of Richmond; Lee's army capitulated; Mosby surrendered; in fact the old giant, armless, headless, legless, a miserable trunk of lies and sins and filth, only cumbers the ground till we can learn how best to bury it.

By the light of recent successes, it is extremely entertaining to read a certain comic paper, published if I remember rightly, last Autumn. It reads:

"Resolved, That this Convention does explicitly declare, as the sense of the American people, (it can't mean the common sense,) that after four years of failure, to restore the Union by the *experiment* of war! during which under the pretense of a military necessity, or war power higher than the Constitution, the Constitution itself has been disregarded in every part, and public liberty and private right alike trodden down, and the material prosperity of the country essentially impaired; justice, humanity, liberty aud the public welfare demand that immediate efforts be made for a cessation of hostilities." The modern title of this publication is, I believe Vallandigham's Platform,—a sort of gang plank thrown out, from the wharf of political rats to the ship of State. Its ancient title was Benedict Arnold's Proclamation.

I think John Brown's soul must have been at Chicago just then, and I think if spirits laugh, it laughed right heartily. It seems so decidedly fossil, that I am not sure but the Chicago Platform was some old petrifaction of the dark ages, come to the surface in 1864; or like those antediluvian elephants, that sometimes thaw out of the Siberian icebergs, flesh, hide and hair all on, and as much like life, as anything that has been dead fifty centuries can be. Indeed, may it not be, that that convention was a myth, and never occurred at all. In ten years its own actors will prove conclusively that they were not there. Take Fernando Wood's word for it—if he write his autobiography ten years hence, and it will turn out that not Wendell Phillips, but he was High Priest of abolitionism.

Four years ago a Peace Convention sat in Washington to pacify the aristocrats. They recommended that the Constitution be amended so that Congress should be forbidden to abolish or interfere, within any State, with the domestic institutions thereof, including that of persons held to labor or servitude by the laws of said State. Now, instead of such an amendment, we have recommended byCongress, and sure of ultimate adoption, an Amendment forever forbidding slavery in these States. Thanks to Jefferson Davis for that. A little less mad, and you could to-day have held us by the throat, while you lashed your negroes in the Capitol.

Four years ago Churches were torn; sects dissected; religious societies divided, until we had a slaveholding, slave-defending religion; Free Press divines; others dumb on the great sin of oppression. It was well, for they branded themselves corrupt. But now who so loud in their condemnation of *dead* slavery! who so brave in denouncing human bondage! Jefferson Davis you have healed up the Churches; taught the ministers the pure gospel; but really we do not know as we ought to be grateful to you for sending back your pack of hypocrites, just as cowardly and wicked as ever, into the company of honest Christians. But never mind—the next moral battle that comes will point them out as before.

Four years ago we had for our distinguished leaders, Franklin Pierce, John B. Floyd, Toucey, Yancey, and James Buchanan; illustrious men! Now we have Ulysses S. Grant, William Tecumseh Sherman, Philip Sheridan; and in peaceful council equally honored and beloved Statesmen. The royal list of American heroes under the old regime ended with Henry Clay and Daniel Webster. The war began at once to shelve the effete relics, and ruling slaves of cotton, and called loudly for *men*. It tried thoroughly and patiently relay after relay of Generals. The American people tender and just toward all their leaders, insisted that each should have a fair trial. Up came from all avenues of trade and artisanship, Scott, McDowell, Buell, McClellan, and Hooker. Each had a full and fair trial; and each slowly sank with the pity of all the nation into comparative obscurity. We needed no more tricksters; no more eloquent Generals. The war growing heavy, and and absorbing the largest armies the world had ever seen, called for men of work, of genius, of unselfish patriotism; of nerve, and courage and piety. And thank God they were found. Abraham Lincoln was not at first such a man. The war *made* him. It gave him a clearer headed statesmanship; it modified his mingled pliability and stubbornness into a resolute will. It converted him to God.—General Sherman has been called out from among our thirty millions, as the one who can perform the most complicated marches and evolutions, and produce the most accurate combinations, and eternally outflank everything, and make his foe feed him; and do it all modestly, and give credit to his superior. Philip Sheridan is given us as the young model of a new order of Young America; pure, fearless, irresistible, and modest. Sheridan and Custer gentle and loving as sisters, brave as only such gentle natures can be—brave as boasters never are; are the twin children of Victory. But above them all, eminent in every grace and power of genius; as complete a man as America has produced since Washington; the man that the war waited for; the man that it would not do for the war to close without; the man that unfound, the war could not close, is Ulysses S. Grant. In these few men, brought into prominence and power by the force of very merit, the nation possesses a gift compensative for the whole war. We go into the contest leaderless, irresolute; with a race of effete, Godless, unpatriotic rulers; we come out having found a score of men, not only to lead us in war, but to rule us in peace. May Grant live, like Washington, to exercise in the councils of peace as benign an influence as in the councils of war,—*the* President of forty United States.

Four years ago, a hound-chased fugitive, fleeing to the portico of our National Capitol, under the shadow of our Goddess of Liberty, kneeling and clinging to the granite steps, praying in the name of God and humanity, could be torn away and driven under lash and curse to the shambles, and not even a Senator—not our President dare protect him. A slave might kneel on Plymouth Rock, and kissing its cold mementoes of liberty, pray that he might not be returned to an infuriated master, and to a grave in the rice swamps or the cotton fields of Legree. Yet a United States Marshal would manacle him, there, in the very footprints of Winslow; and a United States Judge would sentence him; and a United States police force would hand him back to bondage.

A slave might then weep in the touching strains of Mrs. Browning:

"I stand on the mark, beside the shore,
Of the first white pilgrims bended knee,
Where exile turned to ancestor;
And God was thanked for liberty.
I have run thro' the night, my skin is as dark
I bend my knee down on this mark,
I look on the sky and the sea!

O pilgrim souls! I speak to you;
I see you come out proud and slow,
From the land of Spirits, pale as dew,
And round me, and round me ye go
O pilgrims! I have gasped and run,
All night long, from the whips of one,
Who in your names works sin and woe.

And thus I thought that I would come,
And kneel here, where ye knelt before,
And feel your souls around me hum,
In undertone, to the ocean's roar;
And lift my black face, my black hand
Here, in your names, to curse this land,
Ye blessed in freedom's evermore.

I am black! I am black!
And yet God made me—they say,
But if he did so, smiling back,
He must have cast his work away,
Under the feet of his white creatures,
With a look of scorn, that the dusky features
Might be trodden again to clay.

And yet He has made dark things,
To be glad and merry as light,
There's a little dark bird, sits and sings;
There's a dark stream ripples out of sight,
And the dark frogs chant in the safe morass;
And the sweetest stars are made to pass
O'er the face of the darkest night.

But WE who are dark, we are dark,
Ah God we have no stars!
About our souls in care and cark,
Our blackness shuts like prison bars:
The poor souls crouch so far behind
That never a comfort can they find,
By reaching through the prison bars."

But to-day, the blackest man in America may kneel beside the whitest on Plymouth Rock, and kiss it as the first mile-stone on the road to universal freedom; and on the steps of the Capitol, he may stand as shackleless and independent as a Senator,—nay he may yet enter the doors as Senator. Thank Jefferson Davis for that!

Four years ago the black man was not a competent witness. Now in the Supreme court of the United States a Senator introduces a lawyer black enough to be king of Congo, and the Chief Justice orders him sworn in as Attorney. Thank Jefferson Davis for that.

Four years ago, Toombs pledged himself some day to cal his slave roll from Bunker Hill Monument. Let Massachusetts now invite him to fulfill his promise. Let him stand, the fossil of dead bondage, on the granite type of eternal freedom. Let the old Bay State, in mass-meeting, be there to respond for the slave. Hear him! "Bill; very black, branded on his left cheek with an S." "Here! here! answer fifty thousand freemen from old Hampden. Here, by the grace of God, among us his brothers; and that S on his cheek no longer means slave, but somebody." "Pompey; six feet, well built, intelligent—a first-class carpenter." "Here! here! comes down a voice from the Berkshire hills; here, and as free as the air that whistles through the pines, that he shapes by his trade." "George; almost white; his back much cut up from having often run away, and been flogged." "Down here, growls the fisherman of Cape Cod; down here, and when yon can count the sand along our shore, and the waves of our blue sea, you shall have him back again." "Pompey; can read and write; managed to steal his learning in spite of lashes." "Here, here, thunders Wendell Phillips, from among the Temples of Boston; here and a lawyer pleading now for *others* rights instead of his own." And the spirits of the old Pilgrim Fathers, rise around Plymouth Rock, to answer to the call; and Governor Winthrop, and Saintly Hooker, and the ancestors of free American Institutions, and Warren, and Putnam, and John Adams, and John Hancock, and old Miles Standish rise to wave down this dealer in human flesh; this modern abortion of freedom. They wave him down from that sacred spire of liberty; and bid him follow dead slavery, into the dark tomb of the past, forever and forever. And Jesus Christ shall roll to the door a great stone sealed "Liberty to the Captive."

Four years ago a Northern Sheet published the following diatribe: "Abolitionism! This ism has a well earned name. It has abolished good feeling between the north and south. It has abolished the lives of tens of thousands of brave white men. It has abolished the Union. It has abolished happy homes for thousands of its darling negroes. It has abolished the Constitution. It has abolished peace and security. It has abolished the respect we commanded abroad as a nation. It has abolished some of the best military officers of the age. It has abolished gold and silver coin. It has abolished low prices. It has abolished the Habeas-corpus. It has abolished the Trial by Jury. And finds itself at last, like Jean Paul's grandfather, exceeding poor and pious, with little left worth abolishing."

Without contradicting these assertions, the time has now come for completing the list. It has abolished James Buchanan, Franklin Pierce and the like ilk from the White House. It has abolished Hardee from Charlestown, Pemberton from Vicksburg, Buckner from Donaldson, Beauregard from several places, Lee from Richmond. It has abolished black laws from our state statute books. It has abolished slave pens, and cat-o-nine-tails, and gang drivers, and manacles from the Capital of the United States. It has abolished the infamous Fugitive Slave law and the Taney Dred Scott Decision. I has abolished human bondage from America. It has abolished ignorance, and set up schools throughout the South. It has abolished the contempt in which we were held by foreign powers. It has abolished a mixed currency and breaking banks. It has abolished Nullification, Secession and Repudiation. It has abolished all the F. F. V's and the conceit of aristocrats. It has abolished injustice, unrighteousness, and iniquity more in four years than seemed possible. Thank the Lord for Jefferson Davis, for without him Abolitionism would still be in the minority. And now thank God it nas abolished Jeff. too.

Four years ago Jefferson Davis made a speech to the Alabamians. In it he said, "The grass will grow in the northern cities, where the pavements have been worn by the tread of Commerce. We will carry war where it is easy to advance, where food for the sword and torch await the armies in densely populated cities." To day Sherman has just circumnavigated the whole Confederacy, capturing a string of Capitols, and his boys have helped wear down the luxuriant grass in a dozen Southern Cities.

Four years ago, Parson Brownlow was a prisoner and then a fugitive; plundered of his property, and in danger of his life. To-day he is governor of Tennessee; and Andrew Johnson, who could live in his native state, only with an army to defend him, is President of the United States. Four years ago, every man of northern birth was banished from the south, as an alien, or forced to serve in the ranks. It was even good fortune to escape with life, and without violence. To day, those who hanged and plundered, are begging rations of those they treated with savage barbarity. Four years ago millions of honest debts, owed to the north, were repudiated and all unionists plundered. To day, in the wake of war, every debt is to be collected, and every sufferer reimbursed from his persecutors. Four years ago the London Times declared, "The Great Republic is dead." English Lords, with illy concealed joy, uttered many a funeral oration at its obsequies. Now Lazarus steps forth from the tomb, with the new health that Jesus gives to the sorely tried. Is the young Repnblic dead? By the grace of God we believe it is but just at its majority. It was nearer dying when its President was an imbecile; when its Senate contained a majority of traitors; when fire-eaters hurled defiance at law from Halls of Congress; when Floyd was peacably stealing our artillery and munitions of war, we were then fast disintegrating. It was doubtful whether we were anything more than thirty petty, independent principalities. The Constitution was used only as a fetter, to bind us from defending our nationality. But, thanks be to Jefferson Davis, he led off his horde of destructionists. He marshalled them in open warfare. He rid us of a secret, insidious, slow destruction—and we are *not* dead. To day we stand, anticipating a future more glorious than the past, a thousand fold. We see the pure flag, unshamed by bondage, unstained by blood, from mount Katandin to the Sierra-Nevada. We see a people, cemented by suffering as well as by prosperity; baptized by blood to a holier use of its liberties.

We believe that we owe to this Revolution lessons that will be elements of strength. It has taught us that peace cannot be preserved by sacrificing the right. We have learned the value of Union, and a strong centralized Government. We have a sturdier, better-nerved national manhood. We have opened the fens of ignorance in the South, and taught them what we are. The people will henceforth be one, as as well as the soil. We have learned our power and resources; and yet we are a more modest, less boastful nation. We have shown our teeth to all the world; and John Bull, looking in, has found them iron clad and double plated; and yet we have little desire to become a warring Republic.

Dead! Dead! We were sick. Slavery was a terrible disease. By the help of Davis it is cut out; the wound will soon heal. Our vitality is not gone. Purer, braver, truer, more Godly, we stand up to the task of another century.

But to me, looking at this matter from the standpoint of a christian, by far the proudest achievement of the past four years, is our progress as a nation in righteousness. Then we were almost atheistic. Our public councils ignored the King of Kings. Now, however much we may mourn the intemperance, profanity and licentiousness of the land; yet there are, everywhere, individual evidences that this nation is growing toward God. Our coin comes to us with a stamp, that says, they have found God in the mint, down among the money bags. Our President, trusting in policy at the outset, or only coldly acknowledging his dependence on a higher power, showed in every new state paper, a growth in faith, humility and finally, in love for God. Wall Street, that used only to sing, praise Cotton from which all blessings flow; can now sing, Praise God from whom all blessings flow. There never was an army before with so many christian Generals in it,—though at the outset we were led by those of a very different order. Converted on the field too, many of them. Our politicians, with apparent faith, are frequent in their references to Providence. The nation feels that God has saved it. It sees the hand of God in the course of the war so evident that it cannot deny it.

Such my fellow citizens has been the work of the past four years; it has been the work of fifty! We are now really living, where but for Jefferson Davis, we should have been living in the twentieth century. A mad aristocrat; leading a horde of mad slaveholders; ambitious, stubborn; blind with rage, and hate, and pride, and love of power, has been our Pharaoh. God has been our pillar of fire by night, and our cloud by day; Lincoln our Moses; and Johnson follows to perfect the work.

Since writing this sermon, I have come across the obituary of an old colored woman, who confirms my view of the rebel potentate. Peggy was her name; and a right shrewd observer was she. Her chief fear was lest the rebels should get less than they deserved. Her prayer was, "Oh Lord save Jeff. Davis, because he is the best friend the colored people ever had. He is the soul of the rebellion. Take him away, or kill him and things will fall right back into the old ways. May the Lord preserve Jeff. Davis, to keep up the fight, till the slaveholders are so whipped that they'll never *crow* again." Peggy had no idea of our fighting a great war and yet standing at its close just where we stood at the outset. Nor do we. It seems like an age since we began the contest. We have lived in deeds not years. God has made the wrath of man to praise him.

And now, Jefferson Davis, we are done with you! It matters little whether you find your sour apple tree to-morrow, or next week,—or whether like the wandering Jew, God prolong your accursed life, a wandering vagabond, praying for a death that you dread, and living a life you still more dread. Poetic justice would be fulfilled, should some one of your infuriated dupes slay you in your flight, and give you a dogs burial,—then, as the Romans said of King Romulus, when he was suddenly missing, The Gods have translated him to the skies, so should posterity say of you, The devils have translated him to Hell. We bury you this night, under the curses of twenty millions of people; we heap on you the execrations of five hundred thousand widows; we attend your funeral with an army of one million of the fatherless. The ghosts of two million, slain by your ambition, rise from bloody graves, armless, headless, gory, to greet you to the Judgment. All those who weep for Abraham Lincoln, rejoice at your destruction. Four millions of your late chattels, chant your requiem in a shout of jubilee. Oh Jefferson Davis, this world execrates you! It has had enough of you! It consigns you by the unanimous vote of loyalty to the world where God confines his rebels. We will dig your grave in the center of the prison pen at Andersonville. We will build you a monument of the skulls and skeletons of the sixty thousand you starved to death. We will write high, high, on the fearful pile Aaron Burr, Benedict Arnold, and above them all Jafferson Davis.—This from the American people, to him who sought to be king of a nation of slaves; but by the grace of God, became the great emancipator. And then we will hedge in forever, that hellish cemetry, and sow it to all briors, thorns, thistles and nettles; and through it shall creep the vile copperhead and lizard; and cursed be he that ever tills one foot of the soil, forever and forever.

www.ingramcontent.com/pod-product-compliance
Lightning Source LLC
LaVergne TN
LVHW011139110826
845150LV00008B/2410

* 9 7 8 1 4 1 8 1 9 3 1 3 3 *